I AM READING

Small Bad Wolf

SEAN TAYLOR

Illustrated by
JAN LEWIS

KINGFISHER

Dedicated to Celia, with thanks – S.T.
To Sam and Freddie – J.L.

KINGFISHER

An imprint of Kingfisher Publications Plc
New Penderel House, 283-288 High Holborn
London WC1V 7HZ
www.kingfisherpub.com

This edition published by Kingfisher 2005
First published by Kingfisher 2003
2 4 6 8 10 9 7 5 3 1

Text copyright © Sean Taylor 2003
Illustrations copyright © Jan Lewis 2003

A CIP catalogue record for this book
is available from the British Library.

ISBN 0 7534 1144 X

Printed in India
1TR/0505/AJANT/FR(SC)/115SM

Contents

Chapter One
You're Too Small

Deep inside the forest there was

a tumbledown house.

Inside the house the Small Bad Wolf

was creeping into the kitchen.

The Big Bad Wolf was having a nap

on the sofa.

Mother Wolf was peeling potatoes.
When she twitched her tail, the
Small Bad Wolf pounced
and bit it.

"YOWWWW!" yelped Mother Wolf.

The Big Bad Wolf opened his eyes.
"That's my boy!" he said, twitching his
big, cheesy feet. "He's going to grow up
bad to the bone, just like
his father!"

"He won't unless you
teach him how,"
huffed Mother Wolf.

6

"I thought growing up a big bad wolf was going to be full of nippy, zippy adventures like it is in the stories," complained the Small Bad Wolf.

"You're still too small for nippy, zippy adventures," said the Big Bad Wolf.

"I'm good at chasing after things and pouncing," said the Small Bad Wolf.

"Being a Big Bad Wolf takes more than that," said his father, closing his eyes. The Small Bad Wolf pounced on the sofa and howled in his dad's ear.

"OWWWOWWWOWWWW!"

"WILL YOU STOP THAT?" growled

the Big Bad Wolf.

9

"See!" said Mother Wolf with a chuckle. "Why don't you take him out? You can get us something decent for Sunday lunch. All we eat is mashed potatoes. It's embarrassing – we're wolves!"

"All right, all right," said the Big Bad
Wolf, picking up his old brown sack.
"Come on then . . ."

Chapter Two
Chick Chicks

"Where are we going?" asked the Small Bad Wolf, trying to walk just the way his dad did.

"Mmm . . ." said the Big Bad Wolf, "let's head for the old widow's cottage. We'll catch us some COOCHIE-WOOCHIE CHICK CHICKS WITH THEIR WINKING, BLINKING EYES!"

"Can I chase after them and pounce
on them?"

"Leave that to me," said the Big Bad
Wolf. "You can watch the back door
and shout if the widow comes out."

"Watch the back door?" said the Small

Bad Wolf. "That's the boring bit."

"It's the best bit," said his father.

"Why?"

"Because I say so."

Before long they had slipped through
a gap in the old widow's fence.
The Small Bad Wolf waited by the
back door.

The Big Bad Wolf went up to the

chicken coop and growled,

"BUTTON YOUR BEAKS!

IT'S THE BIG BAD WOLF!"

But the old widow's
window was open and
she smelled the Big
Bad Wolf's cheesy feet.
She grabbed a frying

pan, ran outside, saw the Small Bad
Wolf by the door and hit him on
the head with the pan.

"YOWWWW!"

howled the Small Bad Wolf.

He would have bitten the old widow's

tail, but she didn't have one.

Also, as she went striding towards the

chicken coop, all he could hear was a

loud giggling sound coming from inside.

"HE HE HE HEEE!"
"OH HO HO HO!"

"Dad," he yelped, "the widow's coming!"

The laughing stopped.

The Big Bad Wolf peeped out.

"Oh me, oh my!" he said, jumping out

and sprinting for the fence.

"Wait for me!" called the Small Bad Wolf, dodging a last swipe of the frying pan and scampering after his father.

"Why didn't you stop her, you wet lettuce?" snapped the Big Bad Wolf.

"She hit me on the head with a frying pan!" said the Small Bad Wolf. "Why didn't you get a chicken?"

"I DID!" squeaked his father.

"But I put it under my arm and it tickled! I couldn't bear it!"

"Well what are we going to do now?" asked the Small Bad Wolf.

Chapter Three
Piggy Wiggies

"Mmm . . ." said the Big Bad Wolf,

scratching the fur on the side of his face.

"Let's head for Farmer Jolly's yard

and catch us some JUICY LITTLE

PIGGY WIGGIES WITH THEIR

CURLY-WURLY TAILS!"

"Can I chase after them and pounce on them?" asked the Small Bad Wolf.

"Leave that to me," said his father.

"You can jump in the pigsty and frighten the piggies."

"Jump in the pigsty?" said the Small Bad Wolf.

"It'll stink."

"Big Bad Wolves have to get used to unpleasant smells," said his father. "Now stop complaining. You sound like a squeaking door."

Before long they had squeezed under the gate into Farmer Jolly's yard.

The Big Bad Wolf gave a signal and the Small Bad Wolf jumped into the pigsty.

PWAAAH! It smelled even worse than his dad's feet.

The mother pig and her piglets took one look at him and ran squealing into the yard.

The Small Bad Wolf followed, expecting to find his dad chasing the pigs.

Instead he found the pigs chasing his dad.

A father pig had appeared. He was as round as a barrel, with great big tusks.

OINK!

OINK!

OINK!

OINK!

OINK!

OINK!

"YOWWWW!"

"Oh me, oh my!" yelled the Big Bad Wolf, leaping over the gate. "Wait for me!" called the Small Bad Wolf, dodging the piglets.

"WHY DIDN'T YOU TELL ME THAT BIG PIG WAS AROUND, CHEESE BRAIN?" wheezed the Big Bad Wolf.

"How was I supposed to see him?" panted
the Small Bad Wolf. "And why didn't
you show him you're a big bad wolf?"
"I would have done . . ." replied the Big
Bad Wolf, "but he was a terrible boar."
"Ha, ha," said the Small Bad Wolf.
"Now what?"

Chapter Four
Kiddiwinks

"Mmm . . ." said the Big Bad Wolf.
"Looks like we'll have to go to the
park and catch us some ITTY-BITTY
KIDDIWINKS WITH THEIR
CUTIE-WUTIE SHOES!"

"Can I chase after them and . . ."

"No," said the Big Bad Wolf, reaching

into his sack. "You put on this disguise."

"It's a dress," said the Small Bad Wolf.

"And a wig. I'm not wearing that!"

"Yes, you are," said his father. "You'll never become a big bad wolf if you don't know how to dress up as an old lady. Now take these knitting needles and stop complaining."

In the park, there were lots of boys and girls playing football.

The Small Bad Wolf thought it looked great fun.

It was the nippiest, zippiest game he'd ever seen.

All that pouncing and chasing made him feel bubbly inside.

He wasn't so happy when he'd got his disguise on, though. "Listen," said the Big Bad Wolf, pulling a handful of toffee apples from his sack. "Spread these out on that picnic table. Pretend you're a granny selling sweeties. I'll hide under the table!"

It didn't take long for the children to
spot the toffee apples.

But, as they came running across the
park, the Small Bad Wolf wasn't
thinking about catching them.

He was thinking about playing football.

"Can we have some?" the children
called, hopping up and down.

"You can if you let me play that game

 with you," said the Small

Bad Wolf.

"Grannies can't play

football!" said

a dark-haired boy.

Then the smallest

girl asked,

"What's that

cheesy smell?"

Slowly, she peered under the table.

As she did, the Big Bad Wolf growled,

"GOTCHA NOW!"

Chapter Five
Football Granny

The children screamed as the Big Bad
Wolf tried to grab their ankles.
Before he could, the Small Bad Wolf
pounced on his tail and bit it.

"YOWWWOWWWOWWWW!"

The Big Bad Wolf shrieked and bumped
his head so hard that it knocked him
clean out.

The children gasped.

Then they cheered.

"The granny beat
the Big Bad Wolf!"
said the boy with
the dark hair.

"Perhaps she can
play football
with us after all!"
said the small girl.

And she could.

It took a little while to get used to
a footballer in a flowery dress.

And the children didn't quite understand
why she howled, **"OWWWOWWWOWWW!"**
whenever she scored a goal.

But the little old granny was so good
at chasing players and pouncing on the
ball that everyone wanted her to be on
their side.

The Big Bad Wolf didn't wake up until the children had all gone home.

"You all right, Dad?" asked the Small Bad Wolf.

"I've got a headache all over," he said, twitching his big, cheesy feet. "What happened? Where are the kiddiwinks?"

"They got away," said
the Small Bad Wolf.
His father groaned.
"I'm hungry," he said.
"Have a toffee apple."
"Don't mind if I do,"
said the Big Bad Wolf.

So every Sunday from then on the Small
Bad Wolf put on his disguise and played
football with his friends.

He grew up to be the happiest big bad
wolf in the world.

(Though he did have incredibly smelly
football boots.)

About the Author and Illustrator

Sean Taylor lives partly in England and partly in Brazil. As well as writing books, he visits many schools and encourages young people to write stories and poems of their own. "One of the things I like about being a writer," he says, "is that you ask yourself very strange questions. In this case, the question was, 'What would it be like to be the Big Bad Wolf's son?'"

Jan Lewis has loved drawing pictures ever since she was a small child. Today she works as a book illustrator, so she can draw and paint all day long! She lives in the south of England with her two children, both boys. Jan says, "They are just as naughty as the Small Bad Wolf!"

Tips for Beginner Readers

1. Think about the cover and the title of the book. What do you think it will be about? While you are reading, think about what might happen next and why.

2. As you read, ask yourself if what you're reading makes sense. If it doesn't, try rereading or look at the pictures for clues.

3. If there is a word that you do not know, look carefully at the letters, sounds, and word parts that you do know. Blend the sounds to read the word. Is this a word you know? Does it make sense in the sentence?

4. Think about the characters, where the story takes place, and the problems the characters in the story faced. What are the important ideas in the beginning, middle and end of the story?

5. Ask yourself questions like:
Did you like the story?
Why or why not?
How did the author make it fun to read?
How well did you understand it?

Maybe you can understand the story better if you read it again!